Voices from a Farther Room

Voices from a Farther Room

Poems by

Douglas Burnet Smith

Wolsak and Wynn . Toronto

The author thanks the editors of *The Fiddlehead* and *Event*, in which magazines "Winter Letter" and "P.S." first appeared.

Cover art by Doug Melnyk, from his one-person show, "Danny Kaye's Eyes" (video installation, Winnipeg Art Gallery, Summer 1992)

Typeset in Palamino, printed in Canada by
The Coach House Press, Toronto.

The publishers gratefully acknowledge support by
The Canada Council and The Ontario Arts Council.

Wolsak and Wynn Publishers Ltd.
Don Mills Post Office Box 316
Don Mills, Ontario, Canada, M3C 2S7

Canadian Cataloguing in Publication Data
Smith, Douglas, 1949-
  Voices from a Farther Room
Poems.
ISBN 0-919897-32-0

I. Title.

PS8587.M58V75 1992   C811'.54   C92-095793-5
PR9199.3.S65V75 1992

CONTENTS

I

II

III

I

RATE OF EXCHANGE

What *difference* does it make? Well, this is where
You come in, out of the haze of the elms' unengaging
Spring-green. You could want to know what's in it for you.
After all, you've spent a winter out there, mostly in
Twilight, chronic blue drifting, nothing but breath worthlessly
Going crystal. No deposit no return.

You shake your head, but go on: "For that matter
This site has its own rate of exchange. The thought palace,
For instance, is over there, on the other side of the river,
Just beyond the barracks. I mean, there's nothing
Offensive or immoral about it — they had to put it
Somewhere. It so happened this is where
They put it. And we're looking at it."

How can that be? My currents indicate the fictive
Scaffolding's collapsed. Things must be smelled
To be known. These buds' pinkness, even as it
Works its way up a nostril, can't be trusted.

Trust me, if someone happened to capture it
On film, I'd be the first to say, "We forgive you,
We forgive you!" And then you could say, "You're
Nothing, we don't even hate you."

The point being that a rationale can always be made
For your investments: a case of perfume, a few
Toasters, or a box of lightbulbs, a packet of aspirins.
Look at the figures. One thing is also another.
The war's over. Your heart *is* your head.
Those hazy elms *are* your eyes.

9

COWBOY MINIMALIST

I was in Russia.
I was there to play the role of
Lenin, and then
the Italian money
fell through. "A beseeching
letter, a very flattering letter"
asked me to take the role of my father,
and that *changed* my mind.
An admiral's son, an equestrian,
accomplished tangoist,
I did not want to be led through the role.
Any role. I'd decided I could be
directed only by a woman, and that woman
would document a floating
neutrality of me, a kind of
salamander-in-a-state-of-grace frame.
Self-obsessed and self-effacing, watching
my ego fall away like a tail. And grow back.
Spontaneous empathy. Again,
no backers. The calls went out.
Bangkok, Boise, Banff.
I was on the runway in Paris,
a soft pastel trying to find a hard alternative
to my own image, fifteen minutes' worth
of neo-expressionist fame, *a bounding line,*
running through Lenin's tics out of habit —
fingering various orifices
in a post-coital reverie of starvation statistics —
the flight attendants debating whether or not art and
life were one, are one, but the pilot couldn't
get clearance, so we sat there
until the engines filled with sand, and that's how
I ended up at The Crybaby Ranch.
Limbo for Dudes.
I spoke 96-point.

10

I used short sentences, no sentence
more than 10 words long.
No word more than (count them) 13 letters.
Cowboy minimalist.
I loved alliteration, I loved cliché.
Sun in a silky serape.
I was the guide for the guys
whose consciousness had yet to be
raised, who were there for the charade
of seducing bimbos
poured into jeans, who wanted
more than anything else ... engagement rings.
And I mean
engagement. They all fell
for Dante, the fireside lounge singer,
open shirt, luxuriant chest hair, antique
Roman medallion, synthesizer on credit.
How could they resist the electrified
accompaniment to his sonnets
in that thick Valentino accent?
O Darlene, bellissima, spandex-souled wanderer ....
He left without notice with a bodybuilder from Toronto
and so closed the window on Renaissance song
where the vulgar buffalo roam. The enterprise collapsed
to the strains of clavichord honkytonk.
And I moved onward and downward searching
for a smoother saddle to ride out the century in.

11

THE CONDITIONAL RULES

As if the pigeons burbling
every morning at five were time
travellers nursing hangovers
As if the magnetic needle breaking through the skin
of my wrist hadn't been there all along
and the airport metal detector hadn't
instantly fallen instantly fallen instantly in love with it
As if "worry free" service signalled an evolutionary
poetic mutation: the hollow concrete
As if the evening sky actually *were* a patient
(critical condition delerious streaks clotting)
As if a bug smaller than a period couldn't
conduct an orchestra, and all Paris
weren't contained in a demi-tasse
steaming on the zinc just off the Pont Neuf
As if you can't hear this or be moved
by the fingers of a hand making sense out of ink,
out of stroking the beloved
As if hairs that fall don't forsee their own
falling like letters into the metal mailbox cold dark
As if nothing could happen, again, again nothing
Oranges — as if oranges were pencils, under erasure
As if a blank tape played backward revealed
the bestiary of the atom, or the scraped bowel
of a voice repeating   n'oubliez pas   n'oubliez pas
Yes! As if, As is, As if ...
after the bomb drops
a pair of black trousers gets up off the floor
wraps it legs around the Cross, praying
it's all true
(As if it weren't, if it were)
As if coins inserted into mouths of
the dead weren't "tears of cruel laughter"
or 83 poems a regiment of bad cheques
As if biography were possible

As if — what language! what silence! — the tongue
were a penis the penis a tongue
As if the nostrils were Dover
As if fingertips hibernate in the vagina
As if to decide there is Fiction could make any difference
As if nothing will happen
As if this were a personal line of credit
As if emptying your pockets your purse
could make you lighter, more transparent, prepare
you like a target for luck
As if this is where you really come in, the critical eye
As if you shouldn't be here you were
meant to be aborted but your mother had second
and third thoughts she later regretted
As if, alarmed, you raise some objection

13

INAUGURAL EXHIBITION

The integral. Top of the first, nobody on,
Nobody out. Does this mean I can do anything
I please? Brains are white, but we want gray ones.
Gee, I'm feeling very nostalgic. We won't ever become normal,
Will we? I didn't realize I was such a rat:

> The hand reached up pleadingly out of the subway
> grate. I undid my Rolex, strapped it to that poor
> grateful wrist. I do this sort of thing all the
> time. When do I get the medal for magnanimity?
> If this were Arcadia, *and it ain't*, I'd have one
> already. Long ago the great plans were made,
> mélange superieur, by the big guy, great salt
> and pepper shaker of the world, known and otherwise,
> to drive us out/sweep us away in one mixed metaphor.

I stand, I look, I listen. Oh, and I observe
Passover though it does me little good. Fasting
Slows everything down to a pace acceptable
Even to a speed-demon like me, so foreknowledge
And hindsight fuck in the muck of the instant.
The homaged gaze is unflinching:
> We went to the movies all the time. When the screen
> lit up we shuddered. But more often than not we were
> disappointed. The print always grainy, the image
> of images scarred.

Not a bad vision of community, I'd say. Cloistral remove,
Great rooms for the original timekeeping function.

Witty flights of snare commentary, and guys
Kicking the music up another notch. If you're looking
To play with the meter as much as we do here,
You tend to look to the elitism of ice,
Its solo on *All The Things You Are* is not just busy
Grinding but satirical and contentious and
Double visions tripled having sons and daughters.

INCENTIVES FOR THE SELF, DIRECTIONS FOR SCARS

No use insisting on the beginning.
It's already too late (for a victim).
More on this later. Who
You are, anyway.
You can't want to know that
            Yet you do. *How does it*
            Feel? Dig ...

Years ahead, after you decide that being
"Laconic, subtle and full of lyrical effects"
Has not been nearly enough, hasn't produced the captivating
Cadences you'd hoped would turn
Desire as an unguarded barracks
(Everyone but you, on your flimsy cot, AWOL)
Into tributes and transactions,
You retract the blurb of well-defended "life,"
Settling into patterns of speech insistent
As rain in the jungle, each word drenched
With the odour of failed lust, sweat-salt, caked
Along the edges, falling to some less obsessive
Level of expression. Then you can comfortably
Discuss what you've learned but hoped wouldn't
Enjoy being deficient: "I like it fine
Down here. Working with my hands." Working
Against abstraction?   No, down to the token knucklebone
Someone has the mate to. Emotional
Understudy. Staring into the mirror at another actor
Never quite in focus. This is where the victim thing
Comes in: split, wrenched, wretched, delighted. *You don't know*
If you're coming or going. One way
Or another, in or out of uniform, the inspection drill
Occurs, eyes looking you over
Nodding approval, carefully, disapproval.

16

MULTIPLE CHOICE

"Fragrant" or "fragment," I still can't decide which
It was then spiralling out of her mouth, eager, touching
Down on the back of the hand I was going to brush her
Cheek romantically with, but drew back at the last
Instant (even more romantically), pinned between the two
Words I heard but didn't hear (there was only
One, of course, and it might have led to love,
Sex, trips to the dentist with kids), but because
I couldn't be sure, because I couldn't own the one word
That wasn't, and because she refused to seem the type
To repeat herself with lips hovering over the soft froth
Of café au lait, I let it all go: the lips,
The sex, the intertwined urban-vegetable-market-espresso bar
Afternoons, all for the *false compare*, the single's single
Look back along the tracks, wondering how, how it would have
Ever gotten beyond the first fever, the fierce fumbling,
The decades of discontented familiarity, the stumbling forward
Together and finally tumbling into the ravine hunched up
Holding hands and performing unrehearsed together
A perfectly harmonious grovelling throat-rattle.

DUE PROCESS

It was a trail and a trial, as usual.
In the courtroom, no rain was imminent, though a few clouds
Passed through via the large windows overlooking
The crematorium. The hiker for the prosecution
Asked the defendant for *the few choice words.*
The judge ruled they couldn't be said. Because.
There were groans and more groans from somewhere.
(Two lovers were frustrating each other
Behind the bench.) Yes, it was time
To remove white wigs in the wide woods.
Tristan Tzara would've been extra happy.
Everyone was extremely guilty and worked on a longer
Stride. They slurped pine-needle soup
And waited calmly for the sentence.
"For the gutting of ghazals: — the axe.
At the end of the chopping there shall be no fingers."

REMAIN CALM, DO NOT PANIC

I paid the fine with the inevitable plum-blossom.
It passed clear through the pain barrier
That before had seemed so permanent, so impenetrable.
I was dismayed by the strain of mysticism I had detected
In a new admirer. The last thing I wanted was
An erupting volcano. A breach in the moral night.
Anyone else would have gone straight home to commit suicide.
So the police state was officially launched and soon we witnessed
The rise of the detective novel in which no one
Ever washes dishes. Not a tap running not a toilet flushed.
My premonition was that I'd be found sleeping in the open
On the eve of my internment in the third of my asylums
Housing eulogies for civilization and its advertisements.
So much for paying up. There are now no questions,
Just announcements, and flares that light up the landscape
For the midnight harvesting of heads.

19

"THE WOODEN GUARDIAN OF OUR PRIVACY
QUICK ON ITS AXLE TURN"

Keep that rare tone: —

It has the grandeur of an authentic sacrilege,
Of a professional Argentine tango slickness.

"I wanna dance with somebody."

But never forget, Rimbaud was an Abyssinian
Slave-runner. Contagion, then, at least, was obvious.

Guilty in his teens, of dipping into
Maupassant, enchanted
By the primitive menhirs
Which may have inspired the curious
Half-excremental
Forms of his
Brown landscapes,

He walked into the hallway to discover
Hundreds of white rose-petals on the red carpet.

20

OPENINGS

After a while the screens no longer fit, the hooks screwed
In the screen frames won't reach the eyes screwed in the oak Sills so
that at night small moths fly through small
Openings and immolate on the bulb lighting the clutter
Of the desk. There are other openings,
Some with "For Rent" signs announcing them, while some
Are holes in the language that appear when reading late.
The word "moon" will widen into a tunnel a train roars
Through a child falls off her tricycle onto the tracks. Then
There are no sides to anything. Totems become airport
Gifts. Outlets are selling tickets to the disappearance
Of monotony from the surrealist horizon. O gaps, deserts,
Chrome-domed pavilions of peanuts and social theory,
The ways around you should be posted in affectionately bold
Letters spelling the name of the place one must visit
To gather the courage to go on repairing and staring out windows.

VICO'S BLUES
 "Historians are brain-dead."
 — Stanley Fish

Let's try to be justly insincere for a moment. Let's
Follow procedures for the avoidance of being
Someone else. Let there be no mistake
Or notable achievement. *Rack them up.*

                   A little chalk. A little English.
                  In the form of devotional poetry.
                   Slam the cueball into the black.
                   Into a side pocket of the past.
                   The felt's laid bare. Now what?

It's a mug's game. Say it loud —
"I'm brain-dead and I'm proud." Say it
And all the facts of historicity pile up
Like the bones and skulls arranged in those horribly elegant
Patterns of crosses and circles in the drippy catacombs
Under the streets of Paris. Say it right after you swallow
Some sweet poison (it tastes better when it's free):
"George Herbert was a son-of-a-bitch."
No obscurity can draw you out of the fog of choosing, the wheel
That stays put while you run around it and
Around it devoted to its ridiculous stealth and grief.
When you're gone, finally, only then, doth it move, turn, burn
A little rubber in celebration of your absence. It's got
Chains on it for the long journey back to where it came from
Without you. Vico spots George Herbert a hundred
and runs the table.

THE NEW REVISIONISM

It often goes that way, eh? — the peculiar suicidal
Duel, then the historic thunderbolt. Stomping & pounding,
Shouting "I will" & "I won't." No one
Can do much about anything. The needle
Reaching the centre of the record scratches
Around & around. The mistaken provide
A flourish only here & there. You keep looking back
(Not daring to light a match). What stops you
From favouring what won't fly over what will? Like —
Do you think it's wise to be continually pre-occupied
With sequence? This is a school like any other,
Dependent on experiment & patronage & the trigger
Of the soul being squeezed at just the right moment.
Toothpaste really, always being brushed on to try & prevent
The inevitable (okay, so it's a banal analogy) decay from
Setting in. In the dark you can see far enough ahead
To make out campfires & wonder about the tyranny
Behind them. Smoke, ramparts, barb-wire?
Whistling relieves a little tension. Rubbing the elbow
Of one arm raw with the raw hand of the other. You wish
It was only a dream. You could get up off your knees.

A SEASON IN THE MINORS

"Look," he continued, "I also have a big
Problem with my body." Articulated, as it were,
By a resentful labourer, as one who would welcome
Resourcefully the disease of forgetting rather than
Be held ransom by some lattice of coincidence disguised
As future considerations. "I hate to sound self-absorbed,
But these days are like an endless row of beige buildings,
Each smaller and emptier than the last ...."
Oh, grind us another primordial pound. This grotesque
Inability to endure or deny the world washes over us
Like a Rorschachian oil-spill, the crude
Rising to the top, and staying there. "Desire
Used to be a noble way out, but now the cynics
Own it, as they do even death, the dead." True enough
Big slugger, except this objection is plastic shit.
Where'd you buy it? The Apocalyptic Joke Shop? "Go ahead,
Laugh. Soon you'll be down the road looking at your boots."

24

STANDING FIGURES

But back to the game, the resumption of play.
Always penalized for getting too, too close.
Inside each other the pain and
Pleasure double. *Siamese if you please.*
The padded body checked by its own paradox,
Failed grafting, returns to its delightful hazard:
Frozen in the face-off circle. Stops and starts.
No one can score. Go for the big skate. The unendurable
Ice has sooner or later gotta melt and you'll be left
Standing in the corner on old grass or tired asphalt,
Nothing but the boards and their bad ads, the referee's
Whistle glinting in a puddle just outside the crease.

>The salmon were leaping precisely on to the
>grills of kerosene barbeques. On the smart
>decks built on to smart suburban homes. Big
>back yards, sandboxes, swing sets. With
>slides glinting and bare ground at the bottom
>of the ladders and the gently sloped metal.
>Spring, fish, in the air. Wild rice, asparagus
>tips wafting through the screens of sliding
>doors. A dry Chardonnay, poire hélène chilling
>in the olive or almond fridge. All very sexual,
>really, especially the conversation:
>She — "You take one more step I'm gonna pull
>   this fuckin' trigger."
>He — "Do us both a favour."

Eros wincing on the bench. Eros on Injury Reserve.
The goal judge has wandered off for a beer.
Someone tells you exactly what they think of you,
Your elbows go up instinctively,
Your sweater's pulled tight over your head,
Your arms are locked your nose broken
And you can't get his number.

25

WINTER LETTER

mid-sentence: yesterday the white cat splattered red
        headless on the white lines of the turn-off.
        What else to expect from technology
        with forward *and* reverse?

    Title: "Squirrel Pushing Shrivelled Apple Across Packed
        Drifts Into Trees." It's all co-ordinated
        like a golf swing, the power of a stance.

        Everything happens
        outside. What starves
        out there, outside
        the poem, unenclosed.

Some would reverently
say: On one side of brilliance —
    the same ancient light as
    always, passing
through the decanters of the trees —

"shadows ain't such bad prophets."

        Snow
        lacquer, a branch
        without ceremony
    the way the year will come in, doubtful
        courage of birds.
        Snow rain snow
        so windows
        are carbon
    crinkling in the stovepipe.
        No need for hype
        the day's its own
        static
        advertisement.

                    You'd take
(looking through the short tunnels
of binoculars)
guard hairs going taut, a tail
snapping in a nervous white
arc, the depression
of hooves through deeper snow and more
to fall — as signs,
a signing off.
                    As if the light now
                        were broken
                    tablets, apologetic,
                sorry for the interruption.

                Letting this continue

27

TWO

SEE WHAT YOU THINK

It was like a very great wave.

"I wept a little this evening, which I have not done
For a long while." I was looking down
From a balcony of the Hotel Welcome over the white stones
And decided what I *should* do is flutter in and out of my
Reticences, simplified and vulgarized. Go around glowering
At something. How characteristic of the grand neurotic!
But then not everything has to have what you'd call
Noble subject matter. It's the same material in reverse,
Almost. Imagine reading it aloud to the Queen of Holland
As the news of the Battle of Waterloo is brought to the palace,
And interrupts you. If you are badly afflicted by
Diagnosis, whatever revolver it brandishes,
If you go dolefully dining on the essential, unbothered
By conscience, falling in and out of lust, unremarkably —
As it might occur, in the chintziest of resorts, on a balcony
Overlooking white stones and beyond them bathers
In the big sea — chances are you'll become worse than mature.
Momentous stories abandon us in their cribs.
A watch stopped at 10:17, a matter of echoing, reminiscing
And clarion notes, an admixture of thoughtlessness and
Aphorism. Last night as I twisted the deadbolt of my door I
Questioned my fear. Of an act of momentary violence
Though the result is forever? Of sleepwalking into some
Realm no less lonely? No, sorrowfulness
That the specific sorrow is always in transition.
It's not as though I have to go out and fight
Some bad reputation. I'd rather listen to Strauss.
Or Miles. Get in the groove and stay there, forgetting
Employment and the taste of undiluted sex. We seem to take
Our confusion straight. Four-four devotion, when what
In fact only lasts out that act is the slipped beat.

31

Incredulity calls. And whether, like puppets jerked to their
Deaths by pride or resignation, or like diplomats
"Crippled by their oversophisticatedly proper broken-down
Psychopathological metropolitan home-life" — we go down
Tone deaf and badly bandaged. Let me see if I've got this
Right: no metaphors, plural! Okay, so that's unreasonable.
What's unforgettable is the Odyssean refrain, inebriation
And fatigue. I prefer those around me, on or off a balcony,
To be intoxicated. Pissed. I painted a little portrait
Of a drunk as a matter of principle and it got taken
Up by some ad agent, then around to the office towers
That block views of the harbour. No one can see,
As they could for centuries, the haze that comes down and hangs
Like a hammock, a diaphonous catwalk, over the uncertain
Horizon. A brilliant brief treatise on this phenomenon
Goes lacking. Furthermore (that word), if Divus could
See us now. Cimmerian discos dropped like breadcrumbs.
And the candied house — forgive the fusion of myth and fable —
Is the one with the peace tower and gold clock and tacky
Carillon. Be refrigerated, man. No one can be expected
To repress a certain dire strength stirring. If I take
Advantage of these fine feet, it's because Mata Hari
Had the same. A certain art study reminds me
It all came to an end in 1922. The mustache on Mona
Made a professional of her. Only a merciless critic
Could ignore this. You can see that I'm talking freely now.
I admit for a while I lost track of what I was saying.
There was the time when no one was afraid of promises.
Of denying that miracles had rules. What power of evocation is
Unrivalled? One guy's ambition was to break into the museum
After dark with a lantern. It was true —
Beauty and love were sighted at the bottom of its lake.
No one before him had dared to glance in that direction.

(Though my gaze from the balcony seaward
Was no small imitation of that costly gesture.)
What sadder story can you imagine than this man lost among
Sentinels on the quay? He was seven when his sister died
After kissing the family goodnight. Before being admitted
As one of his friends, one had, tacitly, to sign a contract
Of reciprocity. The calm that followed smelled of vomit.
Poetical afflatus. My conclusion is that from the reader's
Standpoint, pleasure and understanding depend on one god
Leaving the temple as another enters. Etcetera.
In spite of the mind, everything seems possible. All is
Getting better if not worse, so the triad of things that
Haunt me — democracy, death, narration — dates much
Farther back than Scheherazade and her lord and master.
To remember the illustrations better than the text, the hues
Of the yarn — this is to remember the voices in the market
Echoing behind the hotel, on and on into the dark, until
The foothills rising over the terra cotta roofs
Take on the features of faces dulled by nightfall.
It's so easy to be disillusioned.
Someone comes up with the idea of a stadium based on
Plans from Leonardo and the authorities insist
On a bathtub with sirens and rubber gills. The gratuitous act
Par excellence is "racial." Is it true that the utilitarian
Image no longer serves any purpose? Hang on,
There's someone on the other line. Is this all? Let us
Return to St. John's, where even at the end of June
Snow patronizes the cliffs. One of these days, we're going
To galvanize. And the French-English thing will be a mosaic
Of teeth. There's something chilling, something pneumatic
About the train linking us all. The caboose is loose,
Which is like playing chess short a knight. Having travelled
Across the country with my coffin, searching for the most
Peaceful place to rest, I have opted for cremation.

At the edge of the best town the sign that says "Right To Life"
Has been dutifully amended to read "Right To Insanity."
This is the kind of toleration that painstaking alexandrines
Should be able to contain. *De l'angoisse a l'extase.* So,
If there is no objection to prohibited acts being performed
In private cabinets, there shall be an unlimited number of
Performances. What is this security system, anyway? There must
Be more than the truth. I must confess, I feel this is as much a
Rebuke as the wind suddenly tearing the papers from my desk. Oh,
Yes, you are convinced I am convulsed with sympathy for myself.
And that's so. But passing through tunnels fills me with
Pre-meditated Freudian self-loathing. (Strings arranged and
Conducted by *El Supremo, Jr.*) A water-song would be nice,
Whispers idyllic. How long they'd last would depend on
Their ancestry. Purple with rage: the only way to start the day.
Or end it. It seemed as if we had just started to talk about
Poetry and such stuff. But that mood settles only when I can
Momentarily discount the experience in the convent. Anything
To keep the depression from setting in. Just a second,
I have to take my medication. I've become a junior partner
In my own physiology. There was a woman who loved me more
Than I did myself (I think) and she would write, "I do
Have the inclination of leaving you some of my work.
I'm headed for Seattle with my discman. Here's where
I think I'll be: 654 S. 3rd St., Apt. 128." As far as I
Know, she left there a few weeks back, abandoning the battle
Of compromise. I'm sure she's having her mail forwarded
And is exploiting the convenience of her credit cards.
They're taking over. We don't have to respond to them.
There wouldn't be so many if we did. However, it is not
Always so "upstream," against the useless current, in the useless

Morning with a stupefying light falling on everything as if
Everything in the river — floating branches, small islands,
The odd mallard, half-submerged shopping carts, wheel wells,
Pale reeds — were ignited by lightning on their own
Solicitation. The boats are in place. The oars weathered
To the point where sun hath no modesty. The cat-gut seat
Will leave a cross-hatching on your cheeks carried
Around hours after you've arrived at the hotel. Welcome,
I've dropped to my elbows, my knees remember one scathing winter.
Such is the fashion of misconception that I have embarrassed
Myself at a public lecture by mispronouncing Pocatello.
I've always loved the "o" in *vow*. By prowling
Through the alphabet, one hand holding your head, the other
Turning the pages of black sounds, you can placate
Fossils. The danger is what's at the root of flesh and not
To lean too far out over the balcony guard rail, and to avoid
The proboscides of tiny, infectious insects that lurk on the
Underside of unidentified, flowering plants.
The largest question of life? Has it been imported?
Is it subject to countervaling duties? Your place or mine?
I wonder if anyone who knows Arabic — or is it Berber — knows
What to think of it all, bowing East? They, at least, figure
That the wind is everything, that it unfolds everything and that
The scent it carries, whether pigshit or wildrose, baby skin
Or burning skin, is a pure, mobile moment.
And what guardian can say it isn't?

★

        I've noticed the palm
Is not at the end of the mind at all, but is collecting dust
In my dentist's waiting room, flanked on either side by
A row of chrome and red vinyl chairs whose occupants
Pay little attention to the palm and much more to the sound
Of the drill that must seem like a jackhammer to those
Anticipating root canals. And which one of us is not being
Fooled constantly by our senses, even when the street is
Quiet, deserted? You know the tree is a tree but its leaves
Are black stars. That doesn't bother me the way some things do.
The colours of surprise fade. Perpetual autumnal mode.
"Singin' In The Rain" is no saving grace, especially if there's
Thunder and you can't make yourself heard. *No reason to get*
Excited. There is the dream of one sleep inside the next,
I know my place, I am a locker of lies that has not been
Cleaned out for years. I play three games of squash a week
And prefer to sit here the rest of the time watching
The circling birds, the sun drifting down and moon drifting up.
I hate Magritte for beating me to the title "City of Light."
I love my mother's deafness and my sister's one blind eye.
There were six berries that burst inside my father's heart
Six separate times. I should be so lucky as to die
At the foot of a volcano. Any day now, I shall be released.
And sign as a free agent. Sartre, eat your heart out!
I mean, this is the guy who said every action is moral and stands
Or falls on its own inherent ethical foundation. But do you
Think he'd have worried about all this if he'd had to load a
Barge at York Factory and navigate it down the Nelson to
Lake Winnipeg before freeze-up?
Doubters, Alice.

Too much of me exists outside myself, if only as
Unsustainably as a scab. It's gotten to the point where
When I hear young girls sitting across the street on front
Steps after a rain talking giggling beautifully like loons
I think enough has happened. There's no need for anything
Else to transpire. Not that there has ever been a *need*, though
Sometimes, just before a fatal error in a big game — the shortstop
Missing a routine ground ball — it seems as if it were meant
To have happened, as if the opposing team "needed" his lapse
Of concentration to push them to superiority. How to make
Restitution? Prudence, Commerce, Industry just don't make it.
Some loser's ambushed motto.

★

    Still,
These divine comedies in white wove (recycled) envelopes
Constitute a decent colophon, don't you think?
We've been over this many times I know, and you may want to
Blow this one off, but the quota system of complications is
A heartrending discipline. What am I, a drought?
Somebody has to be able to say, fairly quickly, *no angels
Allowed.* This is a secret, so don't blab to anybody.
Just into my forties and now this. Burning toes, burning
Elements. Did I say elements? I meant filaments.
"Here's a ladder — so you can climb down off my back,"
Said Nick the foreman whose arms rose laterally
The more things went wrong with the labellers, until
He would stand with his hands stretched out
Like a referee calling an infraction.
"You wanna see some pictures?" asked Jack, who had
Not a single tooth and who drank whiskey and ate
Corned-beef sandwiches every night. Johnny would yell,

"You can shove this fuckin' overtime. All I do is pay
Brian for Mila's hotpants!" I had no idea as a sixteen-year-old
That work could be such fun, meanwhile upstairs the landlord's
Waterbed sprang a leak and the 20,000 gallons or whatever
Had nowhere to go but down, to my place. It was a beautiful
Thing having breakwaters in the bedroom. Please get lost,
It's summer, distant-early-warning is obsolete. Kindness
Is an icebreaker with no ports, promises. Of late, every
Anthology has been called *The Rights of Erosion*. Wilder,
Fleshier, my hands float out of their caves to topple
The commonwealth. I've lobbied for concupiscence.
Protecting your rights and increasing your income seems to be
Deathly important. I refuse to take responsibility for the
Static. Oh, grandmother daylight, grandmother darkness.
Both invincible, both make-believe. If we look closely at
The last named, we might see that during the writing of it,
In the puberty years, the turning point was arbitrarily shifty.
Its enlargement has made me stupid about it. While large and
Powerful, expectant, with a fabulous dental plan and vision
Care, I've failed to find a theme with a will of its own.
Way haul away, haul away the shibboleths: "The writer
Himself probably was not clearly conscious of it or certain
Of its worth. For the substance of any work of literature,
Until artistry of some sort has begun to take effect, it is
But a clutter, a random and wearisome amassment, like bundles of
Clippings and press releases in what is called the morgue
In the offices of a great newspaper, but not sorted or
Alphabetized; like someone's hoarded accumulation of scrapbook
Material, untrimmed, unpasted." A panacea-like way of saying
"This is just to say." For obvious reasons, this has not been
Published in English. It could cause pulmonary problems.
These days, anything could, even the small contrasts in a
Millefleurs tapestry. Do you remember how it starts,
In medias res, in an Austrian chairlift with a frayed cable?

38

The mere encouragement of a musician of the sublime
Laying his head on the cacophonist's shoulder provides a rather
Forceful homogeneity. Bygone time (a witch's sabbath) gives
Sick people bad dreams, fever. Comfortable? Good, but if this
Is a joke, it's one that has persisted year after year.
In 1951, these bookish words spread across the prairie:
"My endeavor is to render the heavy light. Cervantes is
Hysterical." Would you have me theorize about amorous
Proclivity? I hope to counteract the wrong ideas and
Morbid influences of the mountain. If you know what I mean.
L'addition, s'il vous plait.

III

THAT SORT OF THING

Single parent stabs his two little girls to death.
That sort of thing. The school library
Converted into a grieving room. That
Sort of thing. The southern literary journal called
The Exquisite Corpse. That sort of thing.
Here is the information you requested: about the two teenage
Boys out hunting partridge with shotguns, one kneels down
To shoot, the other says "stay down, I'm going to shoot,"
The first says "What?" standing up. The coffin, closed.
That sort of thing. The poet who writes the column arguing
That "real" art transforms the events of the world into something
Memorable. Yes, that sort of thing, too.

LANGUAGE LAB

Grabbed for but just
    missed,
the suicidal vial
    of analogies
rolled off its
    bevelled rack
at the edge of the table
    & emptied itself
(like a bad heart-valve).

All those precious comparisons,
    implied &
otherwise, no one suspected of being
    discontent,
splattering the floor with their
    brainy inventiveness.
Nothing but plain statement
    left to get by

on, so that it seemed
    permissible if not
obligatory to speak realistically &
    only realistically.

Or so it was thought. The box
    of infinitives
quarantine-sealed, the gerunds
    freeze-dried &
the rest of the syntactical

menagerie, neurotic
in their white cages & mazes,
   paced back
& forth, tripping levers, seeking
   rhetorical rewards.

Outside, demonstrators carried signs
   about violations
of even the smallest word's
   inalienable right
to conspire against the literal.

CHAMBERS

He's been studying the hair on arms.
Studying the women in magazines
Who don't shave their legs.
The legs of tables that wobble.
Trying to remember the names of friends.

1700 hours, he's oiling the barrel.
Studied the barrel from both ends.
Fits easily in his mouth.
Anybody's mouth.
Tastes probably like a mineshaft.

The heat comes to him from the South.
Lots of people who shouldn't vote, vote
For the heat. He knows they ought
To be shot. The toaster's shot.
Nothing worse than the smell of burnt toast.

Trigger like a sliver moon.

Chambers need to be filled.
He loves the clicks.

He's filled out all the surveys
And still doesn't need glasses.

Can't shoot everybody
He'd like to.
Shareholders in the heat.
Someone should see his steady hand.
Stripes are dangerous, if he just
Shot people wearing stripes in a restaurant.
Smells come to him from other rooms.

If he could only move.
Nobody visits him, okay?

46

A TAXONOMY

There was nothing to be said except
The price tags of the sky were filling the sky
Quite curiously. Evening was busy being
Overcharged, a furious commerce. To account for it
Would have required a turning away, a turning in
Of the relentless intention that taxed the eyesight.
(The authorities would have had to be summoned
Down from their flagpoles, or at least their horses.
You have the right to remain silent ....)
To put it in print, much later, risked
Disturbing the uselessness of colour arranged
So that its insufficiencies could oblige the darkness.
And in that well-conditioned festivity the silence
Got louder louder still so pleased
Someone was taking it all in, considering the cost.

CLAMOUR AND HOPE

Finally recovered from long, strange illnesses,
She concluded that if she had to be
Baffled, she may as well get creative
About it. Imagined herself as Sappho
Shot ahead a few millenia,
Trying to decipher Madonna, concerts
Of vivid breasts and breathless tenses. She looked for
The line she could really put herself on, coerced
Her own greed, the sensual reservoir of widening
Margins and changeable surfaces, even when
Frozen, due to currents underneath
The sunset light on it. Even in her war
Against punctuation, making the world
Safe for catachresis, she refused to invest in any
Degree of skepticism. She had twins,
Clamour and Hope.
Her adoration came easily after the utopian census.
Added to her resumé, paraboliste, she authorized
Herself in gender novels as Leda,
Prepared us for the privileging of none over never.

THE SEAM ALLOWANCE

She put on the black bomber jacket zipped it
To her chin and thought, "It's all come true. It really has."
By the time she'd realized this, after having pushed
Herself out of the blue recliner, after having put down
Emma, small liver-spots had spread
Over her hands, and a few wider ones on her
Neck. *I'm a museum. Check me out.* She threw
The flowers she'd been saving (they were dead, dried)
Into the brief case she'd used when she made
A sensational, brief turn as a cynical muse.
It got her in out of the rain, though she was skinny
And hardly got wet. She'd walk into the studio of
Some nervous painter who'd accomplished nothing
Beyond what one expects from a decent framer.
She'd drink his wine and patch his dungarees, and while he slept
Put the poison in something he'd never suspect.

49

IN-FLIGHT MOVIE

Digging up what's buried flatters the future never
The past. The long gone, they couldn't care
Less, after all, their envelope's sealed, stamped,
Delivered in a speed-of-light taxi, the driver
With the long-stemmed rose between his teeth
Knows not where he's headed, he's just driving
Toward mirage after mirage and can't fathom
Why the gauge stays forever on F,
Why looking into the rearview is looking
Straight ahead, the road some glacial column
Along the shoulders of which occasionally stand
Decapitated statues of the leaders of the unpredicted world.
You doubt all this? Is the angle of penetration
Too acute? Too oblique? We're on our final
Approach, and inside the terminal everyone's walking
Naked, standing in front of the monitors to watch
The air bus come down with no gear, skid the sparking mile
To the end of the runway and drop off flaming
Into the harbour, and smoke. The life vests
Under the seats rise to the surface, nothing else.
Everyone is strapped in safely, still watching
The in-flight movie. Small fish are beginning to be
Interested in their hair. Their eyes.

FOR AND AGAINST CLOSURE IN THE MOCK-EPIC

The pluperfect hero walked down through shoals
Of decorous temptation and tribulation
To reach a safe matrimonial harbour
In the last chapter. Darkness covered
The malls and the galleries, but he found his fearful
Way around nude mannequins and discarded meat-dresses
With his trusty pen-light, blessing all he refused
To buy. Regretted reverberations, he'd had a few
Too many, such as at the beginning of the day —
Not the end — he'd shakingly decided boredom
Was the rightful heir to horror. He really was,
He knew, the most arbitrary collection of cells.
And this view sent him seasonally from elation
To depression. If only the dragon weren't papier maché, he could
Avoid trying to deny his way out of this imploded kingdom.
As it is, he has to cut his own head off, again
And again, knowing it will grow back
Bigger and dumber every time.

DR. SEUSS AT THE PLANETARIUM

One day the cat *won't* come back,

Meanwhile we'll be stuck with all that food and litter
And the same universe that does unaccountably
Exist, the trillion-billion oceans of years

(In light) we're absurdly trying

To chart. Which is why some of us, like
Cats, prefer to live in the dark. *Not* to plan
For the future. After all, irregularity

Is no surprise. Neither is to hum a notable ditty,

One with the possibility of an endless rest,
Perhaps numbing yet prompting us to mimic
Panicky Angus in his broad brogue,

"Who wrote this awful tune?!"

Which is like blaming the cat. Anyway, it all
Comes down to ... Pick a card any card.
Look, the trouble with observation — that shiny

Black fur, that switching tail — is that observation itself
Always and never is right at the hairy edge of the possible.
Could those be eyes blinking down nightly consolations?

Meow.

THE ART OF THE COPY

Like some born again, translating himself with the zeal
Of a recovered appropriationist, he "righted" the text
Of what had always been "lies": Mary's placenta,
Christ's missing cock. He loved doing it, though
He didn't really know why. Like the drunk who smashed
The windshield of the parked car with his fist, pulling
His wrist back through the matted glass
With a long slice of it stuck in the underside of his
Forearm like a voodoo crystal, and the sick zombie smile
When he tugged it out, dropped it on to the hood
And walked off muttering about someone
Who was so messed up "his enemies were punching his mind."
Which is perhaps why there are no cars in Venice, and so much
Glass and glass-making and rain, whose downspouted gargling
Is infinitely preferable to the drone of competing restaurant
Orchestras in tuxedos that play tinny American standards
In the corners of Piazza San Marco.

POLLINATION

Black and gold fans flick off and on the lilac
Clusters, powdered piano keys falling silent
From one pungent branch to another the way you

Move from place to place on him taking
The scent with you, heavier, lighting
On each new sweet spot, collector of

This is what it tastes like here

LOW TIDE, RATHTREVOR BEACH

"I will also advise his Feet to be wash'd every day
in cold water, and to have his Shoes so thin that they
might leak and let in water, whenever he comes near it."

— John Locke, *The Poet*

Those mud flats he walked along, cold water invading his
shoes, were punctuated with crab tunnels. The crabs hid
underneath, hermit surfers, waiting for the first wave to return,
dreaming of succulent barnacles and the groins of rocks exposed by
the undertow.

Charcoal from a beach fire. Dead crabs, young ones, guilty of
over-confidence, milk-gray vertebrae, isolated thinkers. Everything
depended on the opening and closing of their claws, the social welfare
of their tunnels, the impunity of their vast
punctuation.

55

WOMAN IN PAINT

Although this may sound
Trite, in the flesh she was ridiculously beautiful,
Suffering perhaps only from preciousness not as
A biomorphic abstraction, a brain not simply a body,
An intense eye, a cocoon wrapped around a dark
Vaginal presence. (Tell her you've crawled
All the way from Nova Scotia to be next to her
The way you'd come to ruins, all awe and wanting
To take a souvenir home, she'll look at you
Like you're some creep trying to peek under the stall
Of a toilet, a nasty hook in a ceiling some sultan
Would hang the unresponsive from.) If you crouch down
Very low, you'll find fingerprints on the heel
Of one foot, and being so confoundedly clever you realize
This is a *bona fide* work of camouflage, propaganda,
Colonization. There've been troops here, disguised
As guardians. As a portrait, a gallery herself,
She is the outlined repercussion of brutal desire.

TO AN AMERICAN FRIEND

Incidentally, I got sick the day the war
started. I guess you could call me psycho-
somatic — I got better the day it was supposed to be over.
This was, of course, the least of all the collateral
damage Uncle George inflicted on the enemy, & I'm *that*
too, since the generals have finally learned
how to make bombs so terribly smart
they can find the hole in a particular donut.
          And, incidentally, I haven't felt quite so
vulnerable since Hammersköld's plane went down
in '57. Remember how the big bad reds got blamed for it
since they apparently disapproved of certain decisions
he'd made in the UN, and since I was just seven,
I thought the predicted war meant just that, something un—
everything taken away, gone missing, the hole in the donut,
a head lying in an unlit street, the mouth
unable to say anything, unable to breathe.

VARIABLE CLOUDINESS

The reflection of the front at altitudes
near the jetstream will continue to be
marked by a trough of low pressure
deflecting any usurper-systems. There is
no impetus for the trough to move. Thus,
the front, which is resting in a serpentine
pattern, will remain stationary indefinitely.

I.

Just a glimpse of sun — it's gone. Then uncountable
weeks of gray and heavy silver. Clouds down
about as far as clouds sink.
The likeliness of them opening up, dispensing
massive lozenges of blue? — a smirk
like an escalator handrail informs
the collective facial gesture: "Who
cares?" wiping to "What is this going to cost?"
No one asks, "Just what's this going to do for
transcendence?"   A vague age, and even if
the spectator could play, could help
move the chains 'left' to 'right'
along the field of particularity, would
that make any difference? Would the trees care?

II

Rain. On the pre-fab
slabs of the business district.

There's no

reason why it
should stop
coming down. So it
doesn't. So much
for phenomenology. (So much for revision.)

III

At the edges of fields, at the end of
pavement weedy stubble upturned ground, nothing
is too incidental not to be absorbed
                              into the effect.

                                        Mist,

it could be said,
applies bandages.

Wait! Hold the metaphor!

                        Disengagement brings everyone
to the lake's edge.

Water and sand become Aquaba, the ruins of
Petra, and what some critics would swear was a

    Picasso acquatint
    is inflicted like
capital punishment on the whole composition. Or is it
        competition?   Another question:
Wasn't that a serious band of lightning
a second ago, or merely
       the hint of a migraine? (Pressure so low
it can't be measured.) An aura
monarchial. Dryness. The end of a reign.

    IV

Leave it at: this. The seasons no longer
"can be all they can be." Wilderness, the dangling
Participle.
Here's the thirty-second bite:
oil-rig pumping like a robot bodybuilder
eagles nesting in the powerlines,
their numbers growing steadily says the
man with Orson Welles voice.

Someone could say (if Keats hadn't made it ridiculous, impossible):
    sound perfume, loons through chestnut petal night.

Compensations for gray can't be
declined. Just as when staring at a Carr
the eyes, and therefore the whole doggone beholder,

can't help being drawn in by both sheen
and depth. Of light. What is variable cloudiness
if not chiaroscuro in cumulus? Shading:
Gray water gray cloud gray night gray day. Gradation.

And nothing but gradation, with the odd storm thrown in
to reinforce the syllabic tableau, darker
gray, mountains receding
into themselves. Drizzle-blur.
Slugs on a sidewalk, on
soaked bark. Wasps look for places to die.
The world as re-run:
Have Words Will Travel.

TO FLEE OURSELVES AS OTHERS FLEE US

How I wish I had someone to *turn* on.
Looking back, it's easy to predict
The damage and pathos that arose from ceasing to be
Regarded as a clown. My hands shake slightly.
The trouble with acting is it requires
People, other places, and it's impossible to act
"Waiting" and "Pain." The water's screaming
In the kettle like a bad brain yet I'm calm
For I love that annoying child, the monarch of segues.
Even the cold trees hate me!

THE DECOY CAFÉ

You aren't alone in this vicariousness about it all.
To celebrate like an intransitive verb,
To affirm without approval, as it were.
"You just can't make obvious inferences"
From symptoms to internal states.
"It's beautiful and sad, like the train station
At Prague. Of course, I've never been to Prague."
Present them with a card bearing the word
Peach, and they read *Apricot*. And if you want
To go on trembling in that semantic space,
In your trenchcoat, in that Broadway sidestreet
Not unlike a corridor in a slaughterhouse
Or a runway in a two-bit circus between
The mange of the lion cage and the mange of the ring,
Leaning against the stage door, scratching a match
On the pocked brick of the Decoy Café
(Here a duck, there a duck, everywhere a fake duck), go right
Ahead. But don't expect any poignant finale
With the rolling of the credits, the moon rising big and high
With meretricious captivation. The celestial police,
So wistful yet so resigned, are behind the whole enterprise,
Besides, what's to like? Another spooky restraint?
What's less real than made, or more?
Watch a navel long enough, you'll see it shrivel.
Like an unsuccessful simile.

NEW NORTHERN INSURANCE

Won't, you said, and didn't,
As an understanding of a hand
In a pocket was an understanding
Of wind chill without digits centigrade or farenheit.

And sometimes a bird
Would smash into the picture window
Above the pink begonias in the cute wrought-iron window boxes
Where the bird would quiver in the dirt
Against a tough stem of a plant.
You stepped out of the shower
You couldn't turn off the sound of the shower
On the tidy volcanic beach
That washed ocean salt
Off his 75-year-old skin, the shock
Of water that stopped his heart for the sixth time.

The insurance figures arrived complete
With a courtesy calendar (of grazing cows)
And a calorie chart with figures for fat, cholesterol.

THEORY OF EVERYTHING

It had crossed my mind, actually.
Like some wolf across a snow-field, loping.
I put salt on its tail, just to mix the metaphor
Which is all we can do in the ... er end. In the beginning
Was the Blender, le grand frappé, the pop and
Squeak of the cork yanked out of the atomic
Bottle. Which led to the "theory of everything." Pronto,
Before the first and only experiment, conducted unobserved,
And therefore perfect, discovered it wasn't over.
Everything needs to be held up, like breasts
And testicles. Or a stage coach, the spokes
Circling backward but forward in the dust behind
A team of black horses. They're spooked. Out
Of control. And what isn't? And who, for that matter?
The hurricane parked off the coast — so literally
Figurative, yet we have no qualms about
Going out and standing tall in the unlicensed weather.
Hold on, here comes a famous gust now. Just
Close your eyes, those little engines of theory,
So with the light sealed off the unperceived
Surface goes deep, opaque, and you no longer know what you know.
What is that thing, loping?

MONUMENT TO AN OBLIGATION TO BURN A BRIDGE

As it should always have been, a
                          meandering
reality, a big hymn begun o so many
tacky times before, to reverse the original
premise, the aurora borealis caught
in process, an imagined future
based on a recollected summer
(that one made for wet nakedness)
when the common refrain was
not "Have I ever lied to you?" but
"There are other, better enlargements."
             This is more than mere
                       gourmandizing.
This is Notre Dame in the snow, a
gargoyle's perfection in the artificial storm,
ink on a list of sites fading under
a clearing sky. I want to see them last year.
I want to sleep with my mouth open beside the corner stone
which is inserted here only to keep it all real. (The brain
of the stone is the order of the hymn.)
"We are all dying," the gargoyle said, "except for the ones
in the last sentence."

INVERTED COMMAS USED TO IMPALE THEIR CONTENTS

"There is a ritual who shall say *how*.
You must not ever remove focus-pocus
that you feel; you must not ever add focus-pocus
to what you feel; focus-pocus has a family
tree that won't belong to you; nor can you mother it
or father it. What is the desperation? Ending
lines only for reasons of the paradigm."

GREEK DREAM

It isn't as if it was as if
I opened some blue door

onto the second Empire, bleeding
from the gash under my left arm,

the red spreading across the back
of my white tunic in a thick, drying

paste of sweat and dust — but I'm
not, I'm here, I'm not here, whatever

century it is (who knows, this could have been
lost, and yours the first eyes

to see it in 4,000 years), having renounced
even legend, and she who leaned down over me,

closer, holding my oiled wrists
and moving and being still

over me, ligament and clavicle,
translating the moment of the original and final gaze.

MOTION

Is there a seconder for this — the spitball
Of light at the tip of each branch of leafy
Purple? Am I alone in my belief that
If you're giving a reception for snow, you want everything
To go right? Right? So you want pails of water thrown
At the trunks of oaks, producing stark black-and-white effects
That always prompt a vote of confidence. The marvellous
May not be far off, just over that ridge, in fact.
The ridge that, according to the latest survey,
Confirms it's the exact place Milton had in mind
Throughout *Paradise Regained*. Now it is later
The same century, and the leafy purple
Has failed, almost escaped, the faded light.
Wouldn't it be accurate to say this all forms
A frame, as if looking into a courtyard, maybe
Some dry fountain in the centre of it, a little
Wind catching the mouth of the rusted spigot?
Maybe not. But since this is all I've said so far
About sound, perhaps now is the moment to appreciate
The tinkling bell in the tower, toward which anyone
Can romantically glance and say
"That was sure some adventure. We hope
You enjoyed it half as much as we enjoyed presenting it."
The drifts rise on a point of privilege. The assembly
Of trees is not impressed by the wind's impersonation
Of a pushy bureaucrat trying to get them all to lean
In one direction. Their hour will not come round at last.
What they really want to be is prose, floating within prose,
Or surrounded by other prose.

BRINGING THE AXE DOWN

The first piece of wood
on the stump
to split was maple and hollow

Flies' wings inside
a torn web
might as well have been mirrors

THE SWEAT FACTORY

That it was good only because it had been
Pointless yet full of pleasure. Lips
Playing the other's like an armature.
Locked at the hips, the lovers stayed
Out of forceful stories, peopling their nipples
In partial, armoired reflections. The lighting
Was dramatic, striping them as it came, timed, through
Venetian blinds though it was not a bedroom in Venice.
(Nor was there death there, either.) They did come elsewhere to a
Rubbery stop. Where was the timid brain in, how shall we put it,
All of this? — one noticed, as the rib cages subsided, that the other
Had the word *money* tatooed on the back of a hand.

P.S.

I did exactly as you suggested, walked out
in "first light" with the last of the night-birds
still screeching, so that stones on the path down
to the creek shimmered a little like wet skin
and the fracture in one stone near the water kept
darkness in it like the shadow of a collarbone.
My shoes seemed to promote the coolness of the grass
through their blue nylon. My ankles itched I was
impatient but *that was to be expected*. As was my
tiredness, which felt wholly logical because it wasn't
leading to a logical cut-off place. A little swollen,
my hands were briefly irreconcilable with their weight.
What wasn't expected was the struggle I had with
myself, having to force my face over the water,
having to will my eyes to look down at themselves,
as if I were getting up the courage to look at a corpse.
The reflection, of course, was totally (if not mythically)
banal. But then I started to reflect on reflection,
and so began to feel pretentious — as I do now — because
I couldn't look at myself in the water without thinking
about the *act*, and that got me wanting to stop thinking
altogether (which may have been the intent of your advice
all along, n'est ce pas?). And I began to concentrate
on the sound of the water, but rather than my breathing
becoming more regular, more relaxed, less obvious, it
grew more and more strained and my sternum was burning
and I think I said out loud "What the fuck!?"
I was heated glass. A long paper cut tore
up the middle of my back. My knees were a fable.
I saw a movie of myself falling except I never quite
fell. I ended up here at the desk, not remembering
anything between the "movie" and pulling out this chair
to sit down. Then there was your letter in front
of me, with its advice about fragments and neutrality.

72

The author thanks St. F.X. University for providing time to write, in the form of a sabbatical, in 1990-1991.

Special thanks to Cleveland State University for its hospitality during my residency there in 1990. Many of these poems were written in Rhodes Tower, CSU and in the courtyard of the amazing fundamentalist Alcazar Hotel.

I am extremely grateful to Nin Andrews, Neale Chandler, Sheryl Hawkins, and Leonard Trewick for making my stay in Cleveland so enjoyable.

Thanks also to the Canadian Consulate, Cleveland, the State of Ohio, and the N.E.A.
To the boys at Norton's, the staff of the Alcazar, the Cleveland LRT (on which I spent many delightful and some terrifying hours), the Cleveland Indians, and Lake Erie.

Gratitude to Sean, who said I should go.

And to Angela Rebeiro, muchas gracias.

To Doug Melnyk, my appreciation for permission to use part of "Danny Kaye's Eyes."

OTHER BOOKS BY DOUGLAS BURNET SMITH:

Thaw, Four Humours Press, 1977
The Light of our Bones, Turnstone Press, 1980
Scarecrow, Turnstone Press, 1980
Living in the Cave of the Mouth, Owl's Head Press, 1988
Ladder to the Moon, Brick Books, 1988
The Knife-Thrower's Partner, Wolsak and Wynn, 1989